GREAT DISASTERS

ANDREW LANGLEY

Topics

All the words that appear
in **bold** are explained in the
glossary on page 30.

First published in 1985 by
Wayland (Publishers) Ltd
49 Lansdowne Place, Hove
East Sussex BN3 1HF

© Copyright 1985 Wayland (Publishers) Ltd

ISBN 0 85078 559 6

Phototypeset by Kalligraphics Ltd
Redhill, Surrey, England
Printed in Italy by
G. Canale & C.S.p.A., Turin
Bound in the UK by
The Pitman Press, Bath

Contents

Earthquakes and Volcanoes

The ground beneath your feet feels hard and solid, but it is moving all the time. The outer layer of the earth, called the **crust**, is broken up into huge **plates** like the pieces of a gigantic jigsaw. These are very slowly being pushed together or pulled apart. When they crash or split they produce great shock waves which cause **earthquakes**.

There are about one million earthquakes every year. Most of them do no harm at all, but a few have been violent enough to destroy whole cities, and kill thousands of people.

One of the most terrible earthquakes of all hit the port of Lisbon in Portugal in 1755. Without warning the ground began to tremble, and tall buildings swayed and fell into the streets. People tried to run away but they were buried beneath piles of bricks and stones. The centre of the earthquake was under the sea, and it sent vast waves, called **tsunamis**, racing to the shore. The docks were flooded and the quays were swept into a huge crack in the earth. A fire was started, too, and raged through Lisbon for a week. All together 60,000 people were killed.

The worst earthquakes happen along the cracks in the earth's crust, where the plates meet each other. One crack, called the San Andreas Fault, runs right up the west coast of America. In 1906 the city of San Francisco was badly damaged when the crack moved 6 metres (10 feet). Many buildings fell down and a fire started which could not be put out because the water pipes had been broken by the shock.

Deep down in the earth it is so hot that the rock melts and boils. Where the surface is weak this molten rock, called **lava,** forces its way through and

In 1906 an earthquake destroyed large areas of the American city of San Francisco.

The body cast of a victim from the town of Pompeii, killed in the eruption of Mt. Vesuvius in AD 79.

pours out as a **volcano**. There are 455 active volcanoes in the world which could erupt at any time.

The first danger from a volcano comes from the clouds of hot ash and fumes which it throws out. In AD 79, Mt. Vesuvius in Italy began to erupt. Very soon the nearby town of Pompeii was completely covered in ash. Many people were buried alive and others were choked to death by the poisonous gases from the volcano. On the other side of the mountain the town of Herculaneum was buried in a huge flow of mud caused by the heat. In some places this was 20 metres (72 feet) thick.

Iceland has suffered many disasters from volcanoes. The worst was in 1783 when lava flowed from Mt. Skaptar for more than five months. It covered a large area of the island, and the heat melted **glaciers** and caused floods. The fumes killed cattle, sheep and most of the crops. The result was a **famine** in which a quarter of the population died.

When a volcano explodes, it brings disaster much more quickly. In 1902 Mt. Pelée, on the island of Martinique, blew up. The great flash of heat was so powerful that the nearest town was destroyed in just three minutes. There were only two survivors.

A house is buried by the lava flow from the Heimaey volcano in Iceland.

One of the loudest bangs ever heard was caused by the explosion of Krakatoa, a volcanic island between Sumatra and Java, in 1883. It was so loud that it was heard 4,800 km (3,000 miles) away. It sent giant tsunamis speeding to the mainland, flooding towns and villages and drowning 36,000 people. A huge cloud of ash blotted out the sun, bringing darkness to the area for two days.

The most spectacular eruption of recent years was of Mt. St Helens, USA, in May 1980. Although people had been warned, it still claimed quite a few lives as it threw millions of tons of volcanic ash into the atmosphere.

The explosion: Mt. St Helens, USA, erupted in May 1980.

The aftermath: whole forests were flattened by the explosive power of the eruption of Mt. St Helens.

Drought and Flood

We cannot live without water. We drink it and it makes our crops grow. If there is too little of it, plants, animals and people will die. In some parts of the world it rains very seldom. When the rain fails, **drought** and famine will follow.

Unlike earthquakes or volcanoes, the disaster of a drought happens slowly. It can last for many months and kill vast numbers of people. In 1770, many millions of Indians died of hunger when drought ruined their harvests. In 1877, nearly ten million Chinese were lost in a famine.

A century later, the rains failed in West Africa.

Millions of Chinese people starved to death in a famine which hit China in 1877.

A father and son search desperately for food during a drought in Africa.

Crops were ruined and cattle starved to death. The wells dried up and supplies of food ran out. The region was declared a disaster area. Food and medicine from other countries were flown in as quickly as possible, but not before thousands had already died. In 1984, thousands more lost their lives in Ethiopia as the result of a drought. Drought is a natural disaster because we cannot control the weather. But famine might be ended if people could find a better way of sharing the food that is produced in rich countries with the poorer nations.

Not all **deserts** are caused by the weather. The **plains** of Oklahoma and Texas in the USA were once covered in lush grass. Then they were ploughed up and sown with wheat. In 1930 a drought killed off the crops and strong winds blew away the topsoil. Nothing could be grown there, and the area became known as the 'Dust Bowl'. By taking away the natural grass cover, the farmers had turned the plains into a desert.

Too little water brings drought. Too much brings floods, and disasters of a different kind. Flood water is so strong that it can tear down houses and move great boulders. It can also drown people and damage their crops, creating famine and helping

During a serious drought in Australia, a child picks up a piece of parched earth.

In Washington State, USA, a house is swamped by a flood.

disease to spread.

One winter morning in 1953 a **hurricane** roared down the east coast of Britain. It sank fishing boats, merchant ships and a car ferry on the way. It also sent a huge bank of water racing from the Atlantic Ocean into the North Sea. That night the sea rose 5.5 metres (18 feet) above its normal level. The salt water poured over sea walls and **dykes**. Thousands of houses and factories were flooded and a lighthouse was destroyed. At Canvey Island in Essex, 58 people were drowned. Across the sea in the Netherlands the disaster was even greater. Nearly two thousand people lost their lives and most of the farmland was flooded.

Such violent storms are unusual in the North Sea.

The Thames Barrier, opened in 1984, was built to prevent the River Thames from flooding London.

But in the Pacific and Indian Oceans they occur every year. The Bay of Bengal is often hit by **cyclones** which send tonnes of water over the low-lying land. In 1737 a giant wave drowned 300,000 people. In 1970 in the same area of India more than a million people died in the floods. Worse still, the water swept away the rice crop and the fishing boats, so that many more died of starvation.

Floods cause more deaths every year than any other kind of natural disaster. A lot of money is spent on building walls and dams to stop seas and rivers from overflowing. One of the newest, opened in 1984, is the barrier across the River Thames near London, which can be closed to prevent the water level rising too high.

Disease and Fire

In October 1347 a fleet of ships arrived at Messina in Sicily. Everyone on board was dying of a mysterious illness. Their skin was covered with dark blotches, their bodies were swollen and their tongues were black. The townspeople of Messina soon found that they were catching the disease too. It spread rapidly through the island and then to Italy.

The Black Death, as the illness was called, had begun in China, and been carried along the trade routes through Russia and the Middle East. From Italy it swept through France and Germany to Britain. There was no way of curing it, and nearly a third of the people of Europe died in the **epidemic**. The Black Death shows how quickly diseases can move from one country to another. The germs were carried by fleas which lived in the fur of black rats. There were many rats in the towns and ships, and no way of stopping them from travelling about.

Other insects can also cause disease. **Malaria** is passed on by the bite of a mosquito which lives in the marshy areas of Africa and South America. In the 1940s a chemical called DDT was used to destroy the mosquitoes. Many people were saved from malaria, but the disease has never been wiped out completely. It still kills more than a million people every year.

Perhaps the worst **carrier** of all is man. Coughing and sneezing, he fills the air with germs for other people to breathe. When he catches an unknown and deadly disease, it will spread very quickly.

When the First World War ended in 1918, everyone was glad to get back to normal. But a new and far greater disaster was sweeping its way across the world. It was a severe form of **influenza** for which there was no cure, and which was easily passed from one human to another. Within four months more

Thousands died in the Great Plague of London in 1665. This girl was lucky – she survived.

than 21 million people had died from it – many more than had been killed during the war.

Sometimes good can come out of a disaster. In 1665 the Black Death (now called the Plague) broke out again in England. The filthy wooden houses, narrow streets and open sewers of London made it the perfect place for the disease to spread. By the summer of 1666, more than 75,000 citizens had died of the Plague. Early that autumn a fire started in a baker's house near London Bridge. Fanned by a

A huge fire sweeps across the plains of America, threatening a train and a herd of buffalo.

Forest fires destroy huge areas of woodland every year. Once started, they are very difficult to stop.

strong wind, it raced through the city. Most of the houses and churches in London, including St Paul's Cathedral, were burned to the ground or damaged. But the flames also destroyed the last of the Plague, and a new and cleaner city was soon built.

The boomtown of Chicago in Illinois was burned to the ground in 1871. Some said that the fire had been started when a cow kicked over an oil lamp in a barn. There were not enough firemen or pumps to fight the blaze, and nearly 300 people died. When the city was built again, new laws were passed to make offices and houses safer.

Sometimes fires start in houses and places of public entertainment with disastrous results. In 1885, 1,670 people were burnt to death in a fire that raged through a theatre in Canton in China.

New York firemen go to the rescue of people trapped in a blazing building.

Wrecks and Crashes

Since time began, men have wanted to travel. At first they walked, then they built boats and carts. The boats turned into ocean-going ships which could carry hundreds of people at a time. The carts turned into buses and cars. Then the aeroplane was invented, which could fly quickly to distant places.

As more people move around the world the chances of disaster become greater. A ship at sea can

In 1912 the luxury liner, Titanic, hit an iceberg and sank. More than 1,500 people were drowned.

The airship, Hindenburg, *explodes in a ball of flame.*

be wrecked in a very short time. In 1852 the troop ship *Birkenhead* was sailing for Cape Town in South Africa with 680 people on board, mostly soldiers. It struck a rock and began to sink. The women and children were put into the few lifeboats and rowed to safety. Meanwhile the troops stood to attention as the ship went down, and 458 were drowned.

The most stupid of all shipwrecks happened in the Mediterranean Sea in 1893. The admiral of the British fleet was on board his flagship *Victoria*. Without thinking, he ordered another ship to turn towards him. It rammed the *Victoria*, which sank in only eleven minutes, drowning 358 sailors. The admiral went down with his ship.

No ship is safe from the dangers of the sea. When

the *Titanic* set out to cross the Atlantic in 1912, people thought that she was unsinkable. But one night the *Titanic* ran into a huge **iceberg**. A hole was torn in her side and the water poured in. There was only room in the lifeboats for half of the people on board. The rest had to stay with the ship as it sank, or jump into the icy sea. 1,513 lives were lost in the worst shipping disaster of all time.

Air crashes can happen in only a few seconds. In 1937 the giant **airship** *Hindenburg* was landing at New Jersey in the USA. Suddenly, the gas balloon burst into flames. In half a minute the whole craft was completely burnt up. After this tragedy, airships were seldom used for carrying passengers again.

Modern aircraft fly at very high speeds, and a

At the Le Mans circuit in 1955 a racing car crashed through the barriers killing 84 people.

Firemen sift through the wreckage of a DC8 plane.

small fault can cause them to crash. When a 'Jumbo' jet took off from Paris in March 1974, one of its doors was not properly shut. The door blew open and the rush of air made the cabin floor collapse. The controls would not work, and the plane crashed into a forest. Everyone on board was killed.

The worst air disaster took place on the ground. In 1977 two airliners were waiting to take off from the Canary Islands. The runway was foggy and they collided. Both planes blew up, killing 582 people.

Far fewer people die in air crashes than on the roads. Every year about 40,000 Americans are killed by cars, lorries and buses. Many thousands more are

In a simulated accident, firemen free a trapped man from his wrecked car. Too often the crashes are real.

badly injured. Crashes are usually caused by bad driving, bad roads or bad weather. In 1975 a lorry was carrying 80 people to a wedding near Poona in India. The driver did not see a train at a level crossing. The engine smashed into the lorry, killing nearly all the passengers.

Fog is a big danger, especially on motorways where drivers are travelling fast. It covered the M6 near Liverpool in England one morning in 1971. When one car crashed into another, the drivers behind could not stop in time. More than 200 vehicles were wrecked in this pile-up. Ten people were killed.

Human Mistakes

There are two kinds of disaster. Some, like volcanoes and diseases, are the work of nature. Others, like shipwrecks and fires, are often the fault of humans. Men go on trying to control the world with machines and chemicals, but they still make terrible mistakes.

When the Tay Bridge was built in Scotland it was the longest in the world. One dark evening in December 1879 a violent storm began. A train set off across the River Tay but it never reached the other side. The centre of the bridge had blown down and the engine and carriages plunged into the river. Everybody on board was drowned.

After this tragedy people realized how dangerous the bridge had been. The iron columns which held it up were full of cracks, and had been snapped by the storm. The designer of the bridge had not expected the wind to be so strong.

In 1917, during the First World War, more than 1,200 soldiers crowded onto a train high in the Savoie Mountains in France. But the driver refused to set off. He said that there were so many people on the train that the brakes would not work. An army officer threatened to shoot him if he did not start.

So the train began its journey down the steep mountain. The driver was right, for the brakes would not hold the weight. On a sharp curve the train came off the tracks and smashed into a wall. The carriages burst into flames and more than 500 soldiers lost their lives. This was the worst train crash of all time.

These accidents happened because no one listened to warnings. If they had, many people's lives would have been saved. In 1966 the headmaster of Aberfan school in Wales was worried by the huge pile of coal waste from the local mines which stood above the town. He gave many warnings about the danger of

Many children in the mining village of Aberfan were buried under this landslide of coal waste.

Crude oil pours into the sea from a wrecked tanker.

a landslide, but nothing was done. One morning the waste tip collapsed and slid down on to the town. It covered the school and a row of houses, and killed 144 people. Most of these were children trapped in the school.

The people of the Piave valley in Italy were anxious when a huge dam was built in the mountains above them. Behind the dam was a **reservoir** of water. Some experts said that the hills around the reservoir were unsafe, but they were ignored. In 1963 there was a landslide. A vast amount of rock crashed into the reservoir, causing a wave of water 100 metres (330 feet) high. The dam did not break,

A nuclear bomb falls on a crowded city centre.

but the wave poured over the top. Nearly 2,000 people in the valley below were drowned, and many villages were destroyed.

Humans will never be perfect and will always make mistakes. They **pollute** their own **environment** and make war on each other. But today they are in danger of causing the biggest disaster in our history. There are now enough **nuclear bombs** in the world to kill everything that lives. One mistake with them could be our last.

An atomic bomb is tested in 1946 on an island in the Pacific Ocean.

Glossary

Airship An air balloon which carries passengers and is driven by engines.

Carrier A person or animal who can give a disease to another without suffering from it themselves.

Crust The outer layer of the earth.

Cyclone A very fierce and strong wind.

Desert A dry and water-less place where vegetation seldom grows.

Drought A long period with no rain, causing a shortage of water.

Dyke An earthen wall built as a barrier to stop flooding.

Earthquake Shock waves in the earth's crust, caused by the movement of the surface plates.

Environment The surroundings you live and work in.

Epidemic An outbreak of a disease which spreads quickly from one person to another.

Famine A great shortage of food that often leads to starvation.

Glacier A slow-moving mass of ice.

Hurricane A ferocious and destructive storm.

Iceberg A piece of ice which has broken from a glacier and which floats in the sea.

Influenza A disease which causes fever and muscular aches and is easily spread by germs in the air.

Lava The molten rock which flows out of a volcano.

Malaria A disease of the blood, caught from the bite of a mosquito.

Nuclear bomb A very powerful bomb that can cause great destruction.

Plains A large area of flat countryside.

Plates The huge pieces into which the surface of the earth has cracked.

Pollute To poison or contaminate something.

Reservoir A man-made lake of water sometimes stored behind a dam.

Simulated Something that is a pretence.

Tsunami A giant sea wave caused by volcanoes, earthquakes or storms.
Volcano A weak part of the earth's crust through which molten lava and gases can pour.

Books to Read

Disasters by Tim Healey (Macdonald 1978)
The Greatest Disasters of the 20th Century by Frances Kennet (Marshall Cavendish 1975)
Catastrophe! by the editors of Encyclopaedia Britannica (Bantam 1979)
Disasters by John Whittow (Penguin 1980)

Picture Acknowledgements

The illustrations in this book were supplied by: Bruce Coleman, by the following photographers – David Austen 12, Melinda Berge 6, Eric Crichton 14, Keith Gunnar 13; Fiona Corbridge 24; Mary Evans Picture Library 16; Geoscience Features 7; Oxfam 11; PHOTRI 8, 9, 18, 27, 29; Popperfoto 5, 19, 21, 26; Ann Ronan Picture Library 10, 17, 20; TOPHAM 22, 23; Malcolm S. Walker 28.

Index